Powerful
Presentation Skills

Powerful Presentation Skills

DENNIS BECKER

PAULA BORKUM BECKER

The Business Skills Express Series

BUSINESS ONE IRWIN/MIRROR PRESS
Burr Ridge, Illinois
New York, New York
Boston, Massachusetts

Training techniques, methods, and worksheets throughout this book have been adapted by permission of the Speech Improvement Company, Inc.

Mirror Press:	David R. Helmstadter
	Carla F. Tishler
Editor-in-Chief:	Jeffrey A. Krames
Project editor:	Stephanie M. Britt
Production manager:	Diane Palmer
Designer:	Jeanne M. Rivera
Art coordinator:	Heather Burbridge
Illustrator:	Boston Graphics, Inc.
Compositor:	Alexander Graphics
Typeface:	12/14 Criterion
Printer:	Malloy Lithographing, Inc.

Library of Congress Cataloging-in-Publication Data

Becker, Dennis,
    Powerful presentation skills / Dennis Becker, Paula Borkum Becker.
        p.   cm. — (Business skills express)
    ISBN 1-55623-870-3
    1. Business presentations.   I. Becker, Paula Borkum.   II. Title.
    III. Series.
    HF5718.22.B43   1994
    658.4'52—dc20   93—16149

Printed in the United States of America
1 2 3 4 5 6 7 8 9   0 9 8 7 6 5 4 3

PREFACE

Powerful Presentation Skills is a practical, easy-to-use book for everyone who wants to make better, more effective presentations. This book will guide you through the most important skills and techniques needed to deliver dynamic presentations.

As authors and speech coaches for nearly 30 years, we know that you don't learn to speak just by reading a book, you learn by speaking. You'll learn to make better business presentations by practicing the techniques and mastering the skills presented in each chapter. Get ready to work your way through this book!

Using this book, you will learn to become a comfortable, effective speaker, with the skills necessary to deliver dynamic, persuasive, and informative business presentations. Among other things, you will learn how *not* to be boring, how *not* to be monotone, and how *not* to look or sound nervous.

Each chapter is devoted to one of the vital skills you need for delivering effective business presentations:

1. Knowing your listeners.
2. Identifying your purpose.
3. Organizing your presentation.
4. Speaking clearly.
5. Controlling nervousness.
6. Choosing language.
7. Controlling your nonverbal behavior.
8. Using visuals.
9. Handling questions.
10. Putting the final touches on your presentation.

Powerful Presentation Skills presents time-proven techniques to strengthen and perfect your business presentations. Skills and techniques are clearly explained, and valuable coaching tips appear throughout the book. Learning Action Plans, at the end of most chapters, give you a chance to create and commit to your own plans to master key presentation skills and techniques. Use these to stay on course throughout the book and to reinforce your learning. Good luck—you're on your way to better presentations!

Dennis Becker
Paula Borkum Becker

ABOUT THE AUTHORS

Dennis Becker and Paula Borkum Becker founded the Speech Improvement Company in 1964. This Boston-based firm specializes in communication training with a focus on business speaking. As speech coaches, the Beckers provide training to individuals and corporations in the areas of presentation skills, customer service, management communication, sales training, and interpersonal skills development. The Beckers' clients have included Chase Manhattan Bank, TJ Maxx, Hit or Miss, Price Waterhouse, Gillette, Bull HN Information Systems, Polaroid, Sheraton, and Marriott Hotels. Paula Borkum Becker holds a Ph.D. in business communication, and Dennis Becker completed his doctorate in media communications.

ABOUT
BUSINESS ONE IRWIN

Business One Irwin is the nation's premier publisher of business books. As a Times Mirror company, we work closely with Times Mirror training organizations, including Zenger-Miller, Inc., Learning International, Inc. and Kaset International to serve the training needs of business and industry.

About the Business Skills Express Series

This expanding series of authoritative, concise, and fast-paced books delivers high quality training on key business topics at a remarkably affordable cost. The series will help managers, supervisors, and front line personnel in organizations of all sizes and types hone their business skills while enhancing job performance and career satisfaction.

Business Skills Express books are ideal for employee seminars, independent self-study, on-the-job training, and classroom-based instruction. Express books are also convenient-to-use references at work.

CONTENTS

Self-Assessment and Observer Assessment

To improve your speaking skills, it's important to measure your perception of your speaking skills, as well as a listener's perception of you as a speaker. For the first scale, assess your speaking skills. For the second scale, ask a friend to observe and assess your speaking skills. By scoring both assessments, you'll get a good idea of areas that need improvement. Both of these scales are repeated at the end of the book so you can measure your progress.

1. Self-Assessment

For each of the 25 statements, simply place a check in the column that most accurately describes you as you prepare and give a presentation.

	Almost Never	Some-times	Usually	Almost Always
1. I feel comfortable and relaxed when I speak to groups.				
2. I avoid negative thoughts about speaking to groups.				
3. My voice is calm, not shaky, throughout my presentation.				
4. My body is relaxed while speaking.				
5. I research my listeners' expectations before speaking.				
6. I control the behavior of listeners throughout the presentation.				
7. I elicit interaction with my listeners.				
8. I use notes to organize and remind me of points to make.				
9. My notes are simple, easy to read, and not disruptive to use.				
10. I avoid using a word-for-word script.				
11. I practice my presentation ahead of time.				
12. I present benefits of listening to my listeners.				
13. I use an appropriate opening to get my listeners' attention.				
14. I use clear articulation.				
15. I adjust my speaking volume for the situation.				

	Almost Never	Some- times	Usually	Almost Always
16. I use vocal variety to express ideas and emphasize ideas.	_____	_____	_____	_____
17. I prepare my visuals to clarify or emphasize my points.	_____	_____	_____	_____
18. My visuals are simple and readable.	_____	_____	_____	_____
19. I use natural gestures.	_____	_____	_____	_____
20. I consciously maintain eye contact with my listeners.	_____	_____	_____	_____
21. I anticipate questions and practice answering them.	_____	_____	_____	_____
22. I use appropriate language.	_____	_____	_____	_____
23. I am in control of the pacing of the presentation.	_____	_____	_____	_____
24. I stay within the allocated time frame.	_____	_____	_____	_____
25. I practice out loud and with a tape recorder.	_____	_____	_____	_____
Column Totals				
Grand Total				

To score: Give yourself one point for each check (✓) under Almost Never, two points for Sometimes, three points for Usually, and four points for Almost Always. Total each column. Then add the totals of all four columns together to get a grand total. How did you do?

100–90	Very good
89–75	Good
74–50	Average
49–30	Poor
29–0	Very poor

2. Observer Assessment

Use this scale to assess the speaker's effectiveness in preparing a presentation and speaking to groups. Observe and listen as the speaker gives a presentation. For each of the 25 statements, simply place a check in the column that most accurately describes the speaker.

	Almost Never	Some-times	Usually	Almost Always
1. Appears comfortable and relaxed when speaking.	_____	_____	_____	_____
2. Seems generally confident about speaking.	_____	_____	_____	_____
3. Uses an even and calm, not shaky, speaking voice.	_____	_____	_____	_____
4. Looks physically relaxed while speaking.	_____	_____	_____	_____
5. Seems prepared to meet listeners' expectations.	_____	_____	_____	_____
6. Controls listener behavior throughout the presentation.	_____	_____	_____	_____
7. Generates interaction with listeners.	_____	_____	_____	_____
8. Uses notes to organize and guide the presentation.	_____	_____	_____	_____
9. Uses notes in a nondisruptive manner.	_____	_____	_____	_____
10. Avoids using a word-for-word script.	_____	_____	_____	_____
11. Practices presentations before speaking.	_____	_____	_____	_____
12. Tells listeners the benefits of listening.	_____	_____	_____	_____
13. Uses an appropriate opening to get listeners' attention.	_____	_____	_____	_____

	Almost Never	Some-times	Usually	Almost Always
14. Uses clear articulation.	_____	_____	_____	_____
15. Adjusts volume appropriately.	_____	_____	_____	_____
16. Uses vocal variety to express and emphasize ideas.	_____	_____	_____	_____
17. Uses visuals to clarify or emphasize points.	_____	_____	_____	_____
18. Uses simple, easy-to-read visuals.	_____	_____	_____	_____
19. Uses natural gestures.	_____	_____	_____	_____
20. Has good eye contact.	_____	_____	_____	_____
21. Seems prepared for listeners' questions.	_____	_____	_____	_____
22. Uses appropriate language.	_____	_____	_____	_____
23. Controls the pace of the presentation.	_____	_____	_____	_____
24. Stays within the time frame.	_____	_____	_____	_____
25. Practices out loud and with a tape recorder.	_____	_____	_____	_____
Column Totals				
Grand Total				

To score: Give the speaker one point for each check (✓) under Almost Never, two points for Sometimes, three points for Usually, and four points for Almost Always. Total each column. Then add the totals of all four columns together to get a grand total. How did you do?

100–90	Very good
89–75	Good
74–50	Average
49–30	Poor
29–0	Very poor

1 | Knowing Your Listeners

This chapter will help you to:

- Understand the value of gathering information about your listeners prior to speaking.
- Learn to use 10 key questions in a Listeners Checklist to gather this information.

Knowing your listeners is one of the keys to preparing an effective business presentation. Understand as much as possible about your listeners. This knowledge will help you prepare and make a meaningful presentation, and also ensure a relevant experience for your listeners.

Knowing your listeners will help you:

- Streamline your presentations.
- Simplify preparation and shorten practice time.
- Customize materials.
- Feel more comfortable.
- Reduce your anxiety.

In a national survey, knowledge of the listeners was cited as one of the most important pieces of information necessary to prepare and present a speech. This chapter will explain how to gather information about your listeners before each presentation.

SUPPORTING TECHNIQUE

Listeners' Checklist

How do you get to know your listeners? Use this checklist of 10 questions. It will help you gather most of the information you need to know about your listeners before you speak. Add a question or two to fit your particular situation.

1. Why am I speaking to these listeners?
- ☐ Because I want or need exposure.
- ☐ Because their boss invited me.
- ☐ Because I'm the expert on the subject.
- ☐ Because my boss is making me do it.
- ☐ To practice my presentation skills.
- ☐ Other.

2. Why are they listening?
- ☐ They have no choice.
- ☐ They need this information.
- ☐ They want to get to know me better.
- ☐ They may not know why.
- ☐ They may be curious.
- ☐ Other.

3. What are their attitudes and behaviors likely to be?
- ☐ Biased for my subject.
- ☐ Biased against my subject.
- ☐ Not sure.
- ☐ Biased for me.
- ☐ Biased against me.
- ☐ Not sure.
- ☐ Rowdy.
- ☐ Stolid.
- ☐ Interactive.
- ☐ Challenging.
- ☐ Angry.

☐ Happy.

☐ Other.

4. What relationship do we have?

☐ They are professional colleagues.

☐ They are daily co-workers.

☐ They know my work.

☐ I am their boss.

☐ My name was on the program.

☐ They're my bosses.

☐ Other.

5. What relationship do they have to each other?

☐ They are daily co-workers.

☐ The are professional colleagues.

☐ They are attending the same conference.

☐ They are interested in my topic.

☐ They are competitors.

☐ None.

☐ Other.

6. What do they know about this topic?

☐ Nothing.

☐ Very little.

☐ As much as I do.

☐ More than I do.

☐ Mixed.

☐ Other.

7. What would they like to know?

☐ Nothing.

☐ They are not sure.

☐ Everything that I know.

☐ How my information applies to their work.

☐ Other.

8. How will they use this information?

☐ I don't know.

☐ For general knowledge of the subject.
☐ For specific analysis.
☐ For individual development.
☐ To develop critical questions.
☐ Other.

9. What are they doing before and after I speak?
☐ Eating.
☐ Drinking.
☐ Listening to another speaker.
☐ Traveling.
☐ Meeting.
☐ Coming from or going home.
☐ Working.
☐ Other.

10. What are the logistics of the speaking situation?
☐ Time.
☐ Location.
☐ Room description.
☐ Temperature.
☐ Seating.
☐ Lighting.
☐ Other speakers.
☐ Moderator.
☐ Interactive setting.
☐ Formal.
☐ Informal.
☐ Number of listeners.
☐ Sound.
☐ Other.

For your next two presentations, use the listeners' checklist. How do these speeches differ? You're sure to find that adapting speeches to a particular group of listeners makes a noticeable difference in tone, style, and delivery of a presentation.

Chapter Checkpoints

Dos

✓ Do speak to the coordinators of the event.

✓ Do visit the site.

✓ Do determine the listeners' level of technical knowledge.

✓ Do use the Listeners' Checklist immediately.

✓ Do read the program.

Don'ts

✓ Don't take anything for granted.

✓ Don't plan this event according to your last one.

✓ Don't guess the site logistics.

✓ Don't put off using the Listeners' Checklist.

2 Identifying Your Purpose

This chapter will help you to:

- Identify the two most common purposes for speaking.
- Learn the three modes of persuasion.
- Identify the three types of informational speaking.
- Learn what motivates people.

As you set out to prepare a presentation, you must decide on the purpose for speaking. Generally, there are five purposes for delivering a presentation:

1. Persuading.
2. Informing.
3. Motivating.
4. Entertaining.
5. Inspiring.

The first three—persuading, informing, and motivating—are the most common purposes for business presentations. Sometimes, presentations have more than one purpose.

This book covers the first three purposes: persuading, informing, and motivating. Many of the techniques used in persuading, informing, and motivating are also helpful in presentations that entertain or inspire.

A speech to entertain may be a toast at a roast or a stand-up comedy routine. Speeches to inspire include eulogies and pep talks. Most people do not have to deliver these types of presentations regularly. You may occasionally make a toast or memorial speech, but these occurrences are usually infrequent.

Persuasive presentations are designed to get your listeners to accept a specific point of view. In some cases, you may want a total change in their attitudes and behaviors. In other cases, you may simply want to influence their thinking.

Informative presentations are designed to give information to the listeners in an unbiased manner. Your goal is to deliver information accurately so the listeners can utilize it as they see fit.

Motivational presentations are designed to move listeners to specific action. Motivational presentations are often confused with inspirational presentations. The purpose of an inspirational presentation is simply to stimulate the listeners' thinking and feelings on the subject.

Here are seven supporting techniques to help identify and build an informative, persuasive, or motivational presentation. Review each one before selecting those most appropriate for your presentation.

SUPPORTING TECHNIQUE 1:
Persuading through Ethos

Ethos is the ability to persuade listeners, using the power of the speaker's reputation or credentials. Listeners are persuaded to accept the speaker's point of view because they respect or admire the speaker.

The speaker may gain credibility through a moderator or an introducer. Or, a speaker gains credibility by listing his or her credentials on a program. Both these methods highlight the speaker's status as a competent and reliable source.

Sometimes the speaker must establish credibility independently. If you are unable to have someone else deliver ethos-building remarks, here are a few guidelines to follow:

1. Be brief.
2. Be direct.
3. Choose examples most related to your subject.

Sample phrases that might be helpful include:

- During the six years I was director of the project. . . .

- As the chief researcher during this study. . . .
- Mountain climbing taught me two things. . . .

Ethos can also be communicated through such nonverbal elements as dress, facial expression, or body language.

SUPPORTING TECHNIQUE 2:
Persuading through Pathos

Pathos refers to appealing to the listeners' emotions and is the most common method of persuasion. Aristotle identified this technique as a primary mode of persuasion in his classic book, *Rhetoric.*

Some of the best examples of *pathos* as a technique for persuasion are in television commercials. Listeners are persuaded to wear, to eat, to drink, to use, or to drive a product to get emotional satisfaction.

Persuading through *pathos* involves choosing the right words, wearing the right colors, displaying emotions, and even changing the sound of your voice.

A few *pathos*-building factors are:

- Smiling.
- Humor.
- Religion.
- Reward.
- Fear of needless expense.
- Loud voice and broad gestures.
- References to emotional incidents.
- Visuals with appealing graphics.
- Colorful language.
- Fear of job loss.
- Joy of accomplishment.
- Charged symbols such as flags.
- Emotional music.

Speakers may express *pathos* in their dress by wearing particular colors or patterns or styles of clothing.

Pathos, can be totally ineffective if used in the wrong circumstances. Scientists and engineers should not rely on *pathos* since their credibility lies in facts and figures not emotion-laden messages.

Because *pathos* is used so frequently and is so powerful, we offer this following caution: *Don't send mixed messages.* Be certain that emotion matches purpose; a smile or humorous story can undermine a serious message.

SUPPORTING TECHNIQUE 3:
Persuading through Logos

Logos is the use of research data, statistics, and numbers to persuade your listeners.

Logos is what we see in a courtroom. "Just the facts, ma'am, just the facts." Doctors use certain therapies because of the *logos* or facts of the patient's condition. Consumers sometimes purchase products because they are persuaded by the facts presented in advertisements.

Logos can be communicated in many ways. Speakers may speak simply without emotion. At the opposite extreme, speakers may speak at such a complex technical level that listeners cannot follow easily.

Logos can also be expressed through speaker's appearance. Wearing plain and solid-colored clothing can suggest a logical approach. Hair style, eye wear, jewelry, facial expressions, and gestures can also be used to express *logos*. These nonverbal signals can express authority and therefore reliability.

SUPPORTING TECHNIQUE 4:
Informing through Telling

When creating a speech, one purpose is the simple transmission of information. Put simply, the speaker **tells** information to the listener. The emphasis is on accuracy. In this type of speech you do not attempt to persuade, influence, change, or interpret your message. **Telling** is simply reporting.

SUPPORTING TECHNIQUE 5:
Informing through Teaching

Informing through **teaching** has two uses: to teach without persuading the listener, or interpreting the message, and to **test** the listener's comprehension.

Speakers who want to teach their listeners often use demonstration, role playing, and other interactive techniques to involve the audience. They also may offer listeners a chance to test and assess their knowledge of the presentation through worksheets and assessments handed out during a presentation.

SUPPORTING TECHNIQUE 6:
Informing through Training

In terms of delivering speeches, **training** combines telling, teaching, and demonstration. Listeners are encouraged to show that they have learned the skills described by the speaker. The speaker will first have demonstrated these skills in his or her presentation. Three guidelines for all types of informative and persuasive speeches are:

1. Be clear. Be aware of exactly what you want your listeners to know. Be able to express your message clearly.

2. Be concise. Use only as many examples and as much evidence as necessary to make your point.

3. Be consistent in your choice of language and vocabulary.

SUPPORTING TECHNIQUE 7:
The Motivation Matrix

What are the best ways to motivate listeners? Try using the Motivation Matrix. The Motivation Matrix has six elements. Three of them, listed in a column on the left, indicate what listeners are motivated by: *ethos* (credibility), *pathos* (emotion), *logos* (logic).

In a row across the top of the Motivation Matrix are three elements that listeners are motivated for.

- *Accomplishment.* Some listeners want the successful completion of a task. They like a project to have a beginning, a middle, and an end. They are motivated to accomplish a task regardless of the obstacles. They are disquieted when required to leave a job before it is finished. These listeners want to finish the job.

- *Recognition.* Other listeners are motivated by knowing that someone recognizes and appreciates their work. They do not require major rewards and accolades.

■ *Power.*   Another type of listener is motivated by power gained by completing a task. This power may be tangible and visible to others, or it may be intangible and private. The important motivator is the potential for greater power.

To use the Motivation Matrix, first decide what listeners are most likely to be motivated for. Then, decide what they are most likely to be motivated by. Finally, make notations and suggestions for your speech in the appropriate box in the Motivation Matrix.

Barney, manager of a window accessories company, has used this Motivation Matrix. He wants to recognize the efforts of three employees and also to motivate them to continue good work. He has evaluated each person and decided what each is motivated for and motivated by. On the Motivation Matrix he had made a few notes which he will incorporate into a presentation he plans to make at an upcoming staff meeting.

The Motivation Matrix
Motivated For

	Accomplishment	Recognition	Power
Ethos (Credibility)		(THERESA) Letter of recognition from the president	
Pathos (Emotion)			(ALEX) Public announcement of promotion
Logos (Logic)	(DUANE) A report completed on schedule		

(Left axis label: **Motivated By**)

Use the following blank Motivation Matrix to help you prepare a presentation. Assume that, like Barney, you must speak to a group of employees. Remember, your goal is to motivate several of them. It might help to imagine people you know. What are they motivated for and by?

The Motivation Matrix
Motivated For

	Accomplishment	Recognition	Power
Ethos (Credibility)			
Pathos (Emotion)			
Logos (Logic)			

Motivated By (label on left side)

LEARNING ACTION PLAN

Use this form to commit to learning and practicing speaking and communication skills. In the middle column, jot down the steps you plan to take to master the skills presented. Set a date for completion of these steps.

LEARNING ACTION PLAN		
Skill: Identifying the Purpose		
Technique	Action to Take	Date Due
1. Persuading through ethos		
2. Persuading through pathos		
3. Persuading through logos		
4. Informing through telling		
5. Informing through teaching		
6. Informing through training		
7. The Motivation Matrix		

Chapter Checkpoints

Dos

✓ Do develop your theme sentence—that is, the one thing you want your listeners to remember.

✓ Do use consistent language when repeating the theme.

✓ Do match your speaking techniques to the levels and needs of your listeners.

Don'ts

✓ Don't develop more than two themes per 30-minute presentation.

✓ Don't switch from persuading to informing without telling your listener.

✓ Don't send mixed messages.

✓ Don't simply gravitate to speaking techniques that are familiar to you.

3 | Organizing Your Presentation

This chapter will help you to:

- Understand the two most common patterns of reasoning.
- Learn a four-step presentation outline.

Whether preparing an informative presentation or a persuasive presentation, you need to be organized. Listeners expect good organization in a business presentation.

It is doubly important for the speaker to be organized. You must understand the organization styles that work best for you, and the organizational styles that work best for listeners.

There are four time-tested, easy-to-use techniques for organizing a presentation. Two of these organizational techniques have names that probably sound familiar: *inductive* and *deductive*. A third organizational technique is the four-step outline. It can be used with the inductive and deductive techniques. The fourth technique is *numerical transition*—a simple way to organize topics for both speaker and listener.

SUPPORTING TECHNIQUE 1:
Inductive Organization

In inductive organization, ideas, arguments, and evidence are presented in a sequence moving from specific to general. The speaker presents specific, related points leading to a general conclusion. Visually, it looks like this:

   (x)   Point 1.
   (x)   Point 2.
   (x)   Point 3.
   (X)   Conclusion.

Use as many related, specific points as necessary to reach your general conclusion.

Here is a presentation outline organized inductively:

(x)   Good muscle tone gives a good appearance.

(x)   A strong heart is achievable through fitness.

(x)   Regular exercise builds fitness.

(X)   Enroll in an aerobics class this week.

Note how the outline moves from specific points to a general conclusion. Inductive organization is best used in presentations that are:

- Intended to persuade.
- Technical in nature.
- Delivered to unfamiliar listeners.

SUPPORTING TECHNIQUE 2:
Deductive Organization

In deductive organization, the general conclusion is presented first then supported with specific points, examples, and elaboration. Visually, it looks like this:

(X)   General conclusion.

(x)   Point 1.

(x)   Point 2.

(x)   Point 3.

Use as many specific points as necessary to support the initial general conclusion.

Here is a presentation outline organized deductively:

(X)   Air travel is not pleasant.

(x)   Most seats are small and crowded together.

(x)   Flying is frequently bumpy and uncomfortable.

(x)   Baggage is easily lost during transfers.

Note how the outline moves from the general to the specific. Deductive organizing is best used in presentations that are:

- Given within a short time frame.
- Emotional in nature.

Try This

Using inductive organization, prepare and present a one-minute speech for or against a controversial decision in your office. Present your speech to a friend or colleague. Was your listener able to follow the organization of your speech? What steps could be taken to ensure that your main points come across?

Next, use the deductive organization. How does this method compare with inductive reasoning in terms of getting your viewpoint across?

SUPPORTING TECHNIQUE 3: The Four-Step Outline

The four-step outline is a simple and effective outline form.

Step One   **Tell your listeners what you're going to tell them.** Include in this first step information such as the topics you'll cover, topics you won't cover, time limits, use of visuals, and the listeners' roles in questioning or other participation.

Step Two   **Tell why they should listen.** What's in it for them? What are the benefits for listening? Will listening improve understanding, make work easier, or relieve stress? Personalize this second step.

Step Three   **Tell your message.** This third step is the body of the presentation. Include facts, arguments, evidence, and details. This is where you build your case and present your ideas.

3

Step Four **Tell what you told them.** This fourth step is a two-part reviewing step. At the beginning of this step, recall the most important points you made. Review just the most important points. Conclude your presentation with an action statement. Suggest a course of action based on the conclusion of your speech.

Hints ─────────────────────────────

No matter what type of speech or presentation you deliver, be sure to follow the KISS method: Keep It Short and Simple. You and your listeners will be glad you did.

SUPPORTING TECHNIQUE 4:
Numerical Transition

Numerical transition is numbering the topics in the presentation. Numerical transition can be incorporated with the four-step outline.

Numerical transition is initiated in step one of the four-step outline when the speaker names and numbers the topics to be covered: "Today I'll cover these topics: first, personnel; second, scheduling; and third, budgeting."

Then, in step three of the four-step outline, the speaker elaborates on each topic specifically, identifying each one by number as the presentation proceeds: "And now for my second topic, the important issue of scheduling."

Try This

Use the four-step outline to prepare and deliver a two-minute presentation to persuade the listener to accept a viewpoint on a current business issue.

Prepare this same presentation using the numerical transition technique. Which is more effective?

LEARNING ACTION PLAN

Use this form to commit to learning and practicing speaking and communication skills. In the middle column, jot down the steps you plan to take to master the skills presented. Set a date for completion of these steps.

LEARNING ACTION PLAN		
Skill: Organizing Your Presentation		
Technique	**Action to Take**	**Date Due**
1.　Inductive organization	_____ _____	
2.　Deductive organization	_____ _____	
3.　Four-step outline	_____ _____	
4.　Numerical transition	_____ _____	

Chapter Checkpoints

Dos

✓ Do decide whether inductive or deductive organization is better for your speech.

✓ Do identify the organizational style you usually prefer: inductive or deductive.

✓ Do practice the K.I.S.S. method.

Don'ts

✓ Don't simply organize by what seems intuitively best to you.

✓ Don't forget about numerical transition. Listeners appreciate it.

✓ Don't make steps one and two longer than two minutes combined.

CHAPTER

4 | Speaking Clearly

This chapter will help you to:

- Identify the most important elements of speaking clearly.
- Learn six techniques for improving speaking clarity.

Dis chapta wunt be necissry if peopled jus learnta speak cleara. Doncha rememba sittin an trynta unistan somebiddy whouz talkin bout sometain that sposdtube interestin, but you can't quite gittit cause the speechuz sloppy?

This chapter wouldn't be necessary if people would just learn to speak clearer. Don't you remember sitting and trying to understand somebody who is talking about something that is supposed to be interesting, but you couldn't quite get it because the speech was sloppy?

Read the paragraph on the left. If some of us wrote the way we spoke, that's what it might look like. It takes more ink, paper, and writing time to produce the paragraph on the right. Yet, it is easier to read.

When you read these two paragraphs aloud, it takes no longer to say the words clearly than to mumble and run words together. Speaking clearly makes a much better impression on listeners.

Speaking clearly is not a matter of accent. Regional accents are wonderfully colorful, warm, and interesting. Everyone has an accent of some kind; even those folks you hear on TV who don't sound like they come from any specific place. Their accent is known as "General American."

Speaking clearly is a matter of clear articulation and pronunciation of sounds. The six techniques in this chapter may help you speak more clearly.

24

Chapter 4

SUPPORTING TECHNIQUE 1: Assimilation

Assimilation is the running together of words or sounds. Doncha knowhatI mean? When you speak like this, you are assimilating.

In business presentations, assimilation sounds sloppy and is detrimental to the speaker.

Try This

Do these simple exercises to gain and retain control during a presentation. First, practice saying the following phrases without assimilation. Say them normally or slightly faster than you usually speak.

want to (not wanna)	for instance (not frinstance)
shouldn't (not shunt)	give me (not gimme)
sure enough (not shurnuff)	wouldn't (not wunt)
do you know (not dyano)	

Now read the phrases in parentheses (these show assimilation). Notice the similarities? Try not to assimilate. Read aloud and hear the differences. Don't run the words or sounds together.

In the box below, notice how assimilation can change the sound and the *meaning* of what you're trying to say. Be aware that the more clearly you speak, the more likely you are to present an accurate message.

a.

It was mashed	It was smashed
Joe's near	Joe's sneer
Mother's lap	Mother's slap

b.

That's mack	That smack
That's low	That slow
That's red	That shred

c.

This hen	This N
This heart	This art
With hair	With air
Catch Hal	Catch Al

d.

This mile	This smile
It's napping	It's snapping
Misled	Miss sled
This weather	This sweater

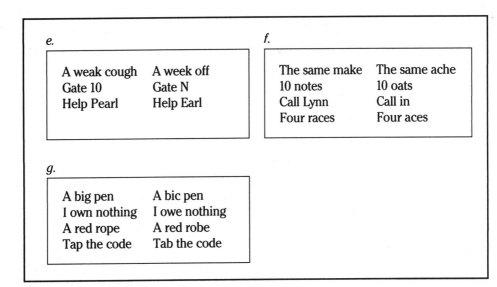

e.

A weak cough	A week off
Gate 10	Gate N
Help Pearl	Help Earl

f.

The same make	The same ache
10 notes	10 oats
Call Lynn	Call in
Four races	Four aces

g.

A big pen	A bic pen
I own nothing	I owe nothing
A red rope	A red robe
Tap the code	Tab the code

4

SUPPORTING TECHNIQUE 2: Plosive Sounds

Plosive sounds are sounds made by building up air pressure in the mouth, closing off the pressure, then exploding the sound. There are eight plosive sounds: **b** as in **b**oy, **d** as in **d**og, **g** as in **g**irl, **j** as in **j**ump, **p** as in **p**ut, **t** as in **t**oy, **k** as in **k**ite, and **ch** as in **ch**ild.

Inappropriate use of plosive sounds poses one of the most common problems for speakers.

Many speakers say that "they prefer to si_ not stan_ when they spea_." Dropping plosive sounds off word endings is so common most listeners understand that speakers really mean "They prefer to si<u>t</u> not stan<u>d</u> when they spea<u>k</u>." Plosive sounds are sometimes dropped from the middle of words such as "te_nical" instead of "te<u>ch</u>nical" or "bla_board" instead of "bla<u>ck</u>board." Dropping plosive sounds like this is called imploding.

What's going on? Speakers intend to explode the plosive sound but implode it instead. No air pressure or sound is released. Listeners are expected to simply fill in the missing sounds.

Learn to use plosive sounds to emphasize particular words.

4

◼ Try This

Purposely explode and overemphasize every plosive sound in these sentences as you read them aloud. Doing so will increase your sensitivity to speaking clearly. Don't worry if you feel odd or self-conscious completing this exercise. The payoff—speaking clearly—will be well worth it. Use a tape recorder. As you play back your recording, underline each plosive sound you missed. Then, repeat the exercise.

1. Pat took the hot dogs and ate 10 of them.
2. Bob bet that he could tip the streetcar into the camp pool.
3. At midnight, the old dame mounted her magic carpet and took off.
4. The topmost blackboard fell on the white table.
5. The black bat and the pink beetle often hid near the backyard.
6. Peter Porter the pumpkin eater had a wife named Dot Bud.
7. Ed and Tod would not permit back talk from spoiled kids.
8. Oh, it's nice to get up at eight, but it's nicer to stay in bed.
9. A man must not swallow more beliefs than he can digest.
10. If you do not think about the future, you cannot have one.

SUPPORTING TECHNIQUE 3:
Rate of Speed

Rate of speed refers to the number of words per minute that a speaker says. Too many words per minute or too few words per minute can be very distracting to the listeners, but a speaker who never varies the rate of speed of speaking can easily put listeners to sleep.

Effective speakers change their rate of speed to fit their purpose, their content, their listeners, and their own personal style. Speakers should evaluate these variables carefully for each speaking situation. *The most effective rate of speed for a business presentation is between 175–190 words per minute.* This will vary according to need.

Try This ─────────────────────────────

Practice controlling your rate of speed by reading this paragraph into a tape recorder. Play it back to decide how you like it. Try it again a little faster, then again a little more slowly. This will help you get the feel for your rate of speed of speaking. This paragraph contains 176 words. Try to read it in one minute.

As the report progressed, it became clear that keeping on schedule would be directly related to the ability of the project manager to communicate with the client. Originally, it was thought that weekly meetings would suffice. It quickly became evident that daily communication would be necessary in the later stages of the work. However, travel and distance, unforeseen complications, cost, and even personality emerged as modifying variables. Personality and the individual differences in communication style became key stumbling blocks to the project's progress. The project manager preferred to make a quick phone call and relate the overall progress for the day. The client preferred a more detailed report of specific aspects of the daily tasks. These differences in communication style caused irritations and misunderstandings. These often led to indecision and delay, which created havoc with the schedule and increased the budget. Eventually, it was decided that both the project manager and the client would allow their "next-in-charge" to handle the daily discussions. They got along fine and the project was finished within the budget.

SUPPORTING TECHNIQUE 4: Pace

Pace is the speed at which a speaker presents different topics or thoughts within a topic. The "best" pace for business presentations is unknown since listeners' and speakers' interest and familiarity with the subject of a speech will vary. The speaker needs to adjust the pace to address these variations.

Business listeners prefer a fairly fast pace. However, it can be annoying to take notes, formulate questions, keep information organized, and evaluate ideas if the speaker is whizzing along too quickly. The speaker must judge how much time to allow between topics and different thoughts since listeners may be hearing the ideas in your speech for the first time.

To determine how long to pause for pacing use the following guidelines:

When Presenting	Pause Approximately
Very familiar topics	:01 second
Familiar topics	:02 seconds
New topics	:03 seconds
Very new topics	:04 seconds

SUPPORTING TECHNIQUE 5: Articulation

Articulation is the production of individual sounds. There are more than 50 sounds in English. When you produce any of them, you are articulating. (Don't confuse articulation with *pronunciation*—you are combining individually articulated sounds to make an understandable word.)

Children learn to articulate by hearing and imitating adults, and in school with teachers and other students. Adult articulation reflects these and other influences. Unfortunately these influences have resulted in mumbling and unclear speech in some adults.

Practice these articulation exercises to improve and gain control over the sound and clarity of your speech.

1. Open your mouth wide and close it. Don't be afraid to open your mouth wide; this is a stretching exercise (5 times).

2. Round your lips and protrude them as far as you can and practice the sound "oo" (5 times).

3. Spread your lips back in a *big* smile. Feel the muscles pulling around your chin and neck area. Practice the sound "e" (5 times). Then practice the sounds "e-o" (10 times).

4. Thrust your upper lip forward. Thrust your lower lip forward (5 times).

5. Stretch your upper lip down. Stretch your bottom lip up (5 times).

6. Raise the right side of your mouth. Raise the left side of your mouth. Be sure your whole face is involved in the movement. It is necessary to have the muscles of your face move freely for expression (5 times).

7. Protrude your tongue without touching your top or bottom lip. This will be helpful for production of sounds such as "th" (10 times).

8. Point the tip of your tongue up and touch your top lip, then the right corner of your mouth, then the left, then point it down towards your chin (10 times).

9. Rotate your tongue around the inside of your mouth over your upper teeth, then your bottom teeth (10 times).

10. Raise the tip of your tongue and touch the gumridge behind your upper front teeth slowly bring it back toward your soft palate (10 times).

11. Let the tip of your tongue touch the roof of your mouth. Flap it up and down making sure you produce a strong "lah, lah, lah, nah, nah, nah" (10 times).

12. Practice *A-E-I-O-U*, opening your mouth as wide as you can using the articulators to the point that you feel a tingling sensation (10 times).

SUPPORTING TECHNIQUE 6: Inflection

Inflection is emphasis placed on a word to create meaning. Varying inflection is extremely useful to prevent monotonous presentations.

People will often say that a speaker was monotone. Since human voice doesn't actually produce a monotone, what is heard is a *monopattern*, in which several elements of speech and voice are unchanging. This can make a speaker sound boring. A speaker whose monopattern is consistent enough can truly put people to sleep. The effective use of inflection can prevent this.

Inflection at the end of a sentence can be steady or go up, or down. As you can see below, inflection can change meaning.

Read this sentence each way:

Straight (Factual)   This page contains a lot of words.
Up (Question)   This page contains a lot of words.
Down (Emphatic)   This page contains a lot of words.

You can also vary inflection to make your speech more interesting. Be careful, though, not to give mixed messages to your listeners. For example, don't up-inflect, implying a question or uncertainty, when you should down-inflect, implying conviction and strength.

Try This

Tape yourself saying these sentences. Notice and control the differences in inflection and meaning. Try to use the inflection and meaning given in parentheses after each sentence.

1. Good speech is good business. (Straight–factual.)
2. Mixed messages can cost more than money. (Down–emphatic.)
3. Leadership is a learned skill. (Up–question.)
4. Fear of speaking can be controlled. (Down–emphatic.)
5. This meeting will conclude in two hours. (Up–question.)

"Did you eat yet?" "No, you?" "Do you want to?"

LEARNING ACTION PLAN

Use this form to commit to learning and practicing speaking and communication skills. In the middle column, jot down the steps you plan to take to master the skills presented. Set a date for completion of these steps.

LEARNING ACTION PLAN		
Skill: Speaking Clearly		
Technique	**Action to Take**	**Date Due**
1. Assimilation	_____ _____	
2. Plosives	_____ _____	
3. Rate of speed	_____ _____	
4. Pace	_____ _____	
5. Articulation	_____ _____	
6. Inflection	_____ _____	

Chapter Checkpoints

Dos

✓ Do listen to yourself carefully.

✓ Do be self-critical.

✓ Do practice with a tape recorder.

✓ Do practice out loud.

Don'ts

✓ Don't simply say, "Well, that's the way I talk."

✓ Don't practice silently.

✓ Don't think no one will notice.

CHAPTER

5 | Controlling Nervousness

This chapter will help you to:

- Understand the psychological and physiological elements of speaking fear.
- Learn how to control nervousness using three techniques.

"It's normal." "It's all in your mind." "Don't worry about it." Have you heard these comments from people who are trying to help you live with your nervousness about speaking? It's nice of them to be concerned, but it usually doesn't help.

It's normal. Nervousness certainly is common, but that doesn't make it normal. It isn't "normal" in everyday life to walk around with sweaty palms, shaky knees, a jittery stomach, a shaky voice, and trembling hands unless, that is, you're worried about an upcoming speaking event. There is no doubt about the reality of negative thinking.

It isn't all in your mind.

Fear of speaking is a very real experience with psychological and physiological symptoms.

Don't worry about it. This may actually be the best advice. Worry is like a rocking chair. It gives you something to do but it doesn't get you anywhere. Don't worry—do something about your fears.

This chapter is about how to control your nervousness.

SUPPORTING TECHNIQUE 1: ABCs of Fear

Most speakers who suffer from fear and nervousness describe their feelings in the following manner:

"I'm fine until I have to stand up in front of people. Then, my knees start shaking."

"As soon as I start thinking about all those people looking at me, my heart starts beating faster."

"If I have to use visual aid equipment, my hands shake."

These examples may sound familiar if you suffer from this fear. Did you notice the pattern in each example? It's the ABC pattern. First what activates the fear, A:

Standing up in front of people.

People staring at me.

Using visual aid equipment.

Then the consequence of the fear, C:

Knees starting to shake.

Heart starts beating faster.

Hands shaking.

The conclusion is, A causes C. However, A doesn't really cause C. B, the belief about what will happen because of A, is what causes C. B consists of all the negative thoughts and experiences you have about doing A. These beliefs may or may not be real, but they are strong enough to produce fear.

Fortunately, there are ways to control the ABC effect:

- **First**, identify your As. What are the specific circumstances that activate your fear? Be specific. Don't be shy. You may have several As.
- **Second**, debate your Bs. Conduct a rational debate with yourself over the real and perceived results of each B you identify. Be honest. Why do you believe each B? What started each B? What reinforces each B?
- **Third**, develop speaking techniques to control each A. Start with the techniques in this book.
- **Finally**, practice your new techniques until you can truly believe that you are in control of each A. That conviction will come from the real control of each technique and activating circumstance.

SUPPORTING TECHNIQUE 2:
Diaphragmatic Breathing

People breathe three ways:

Clavicular—heavy panting usually seen following a run or an exercise workout.

Diaphragmatic—natural method with the body at ease. The diaphragm, located at your midsection above the belt line, moves out when you breathe in and in when you breathe out.

Upper Thoracic—a shallow form of breathing that supports upper body activities such as waving, lifting, and throwing. The thorax, or chest cavity, moves up and expands as you inhale.

Only diaphragmatic breathing is appropriate for speaking. Upper thoracic breathing creates pressure in the upper chest that does not promote the calm or support needed for effective speaking. Only diaphragmatic breathing will provide that support.

5

Try This

Diaphragmatic Breathing Exercises

1. Sit or stand comfortably in front of a mirror, if possible, so you can observe the process.

2. Use your fingertips to push lightly on your diaphragm. Feel the movement as you breathe.

3. Inhale slowly through nose or mouth. Feel the diaphragm push out. Shoulders or upper chest should not move.

4. Hold this inhalation for three seconds.

5. As you exhale, count to 20 by saying, "one by one, two by two, three by three," until you reach 20.

6. Stop wherever you are when exhalation becomes a strain.

7. If you do not reach 20 on one breath, repeat this exercise 10 times. Do this three times daily until you reach 20 comfortably.

5

SUPPORTING TECHNIQUE 3:
The 10-Second Relaxer

If diaphragmatic breathing is somehow evading you as you start to speak, here is a simple, quick technique, known as the 10-second relaxer, for relieving the physical symptoms of nervousness.

Follow these steps for the 10-second relaxer whenever you feel nervous before speaking.

1. Point your chin toward your chest and watch your midsection move in and out as you breathe using diaphragmatic breathing.

2. Tightly squeeze the thumb and index fingertips together on each hand.

3. At the same time, inhale deeply while silently affirming, "I am in control."

4. Exhale slowly, releasing tension in the fingers while concluding the affirmation, "and I am relaxed and ready."

5. Repeat this exercise three times as you visualize yourself successfully completing your presentation.

LEARNING ACTION PLAN

Use this form to commit to learning and practicing speaking and communication skills. In the middle column, jot down the steps you plan to take to master the skills presented. Set a date for completion of these steps.

5

LEARNING ACTION PLAN		
Skill: Controlling Nervousness		
Technique	Action to Take	Date Due
1. Understanding the ABCs of fear	_____ _____	
2. Diaphragmatic breathing	_____ _____	
3. The 10-second relaxer	_____ _____	

Chapter Checkpoints

Dos

✓ Do understand that fear has two elements: psychological and physiological.

✓ Do understand that both elements can be controlled.

✓ Do identify the specific circumstances which trigger the fear.

✓ Do practice diaphragmatic breathing.

Don'ts

✓ Don't give up!

✓ Don't accept fear and nervousness as facts of life.

✓ Don't try to trick yourself.

6 | Choosing Language

This chapter will help you to:

- Understand the impact of language in presentations.
- Learn the six Cs of language.
- Use language as a speaking tool.

Have you heard the proverb, "Kind words last longer than the wealth of the world"? It also applies to unkind words. Many can still hear negative, critical, or harsh words spoken years ago. They can hit hard and stay.

An effective business presentation is based on the careful choice of words to introduce ideas. The language you use to convey content in a business presentation is especially critical. Poor grammar, weak word selection, or confusing sentence construction can easily mislead listeners.

There is no one specific and correct way to express thoughts. Think of choosing effective language, rather than correct language. This approach carries significant responsibility. It doesn't mean that you can say whatever you want. The general rules of civility, politeness, and decorum apply.

Here are six techniques for choosing effective language. Remember them as the six Cs.

SUPPORTING TECHNIQUE 1: Be Clear

Keep your language simple. Use familiar, everyday words. Construct simple declarative sentences. Straightforward speech is an asset in speaking on difficult or complex subjects. Simple, familiar language is most important when discussing technical information with nontechnical people. What is commonplace language to you may be unknown to your listeners. Avoid slang, jargon, or technical wording.

Here are some examples.

Not clear: Research indicates that product identification coupled with amplification and communication concepts congruent with community mores through simultaneous electronic media exposure will enhance bottom-line volume.

Clear: Effective advertising creates profit.

Not clear: The financial stream produced through revenue enhancers activated as a result of recent legislation will supply individual remuneration of program participants.

Clear: Program participants will be paid with tax dollars.

Try This

Take a statement from a politician, a medical professional, or a computer expert. Rewrite the statement using simple, clear language.

SUPPORTING TECHNIQUE 2: Be Colorful

Being colorful means using words that create an impression or enhance meaning. They are called *color* words. They can change ordinary, straightforward, black-and-white information into colorful and memorable messages. This can be accomplished by using a conversational style of speaking. It helps listeners identify meaning as well as enjoy your speaking. Some examples follow.

Not colorful: The conference and workshops produced a positive response from the participants.

Colorful: Everyone who attended the sessions had a great time.

Not colorful: The speaker's obvious rhetorical adeptness promoted positive reactions from listeners.

Colorful: Listeners were delighted by the speaker's enthusiastic skill and comfortable style in dealing with the topic.

Try This

Choose three products and describe each one in colorful language that would entice people to buy these items.

SUPPORTING TECHNIQUE 3: Be Concrete

Concrete language is specific language that expresses your meaning directly. Avoid language that is vague or too general. Vague, tentative language can produce misunderstanding, frustration, and errors. Be concrete. Be specific. Here are some examples.

Not concrete: I hope I have shown you several reasons for the deficit.

Concrete: I have shown you three reasons for the deficit.

Not concrete: I think the next step you might want to consider is to visit the site.

Concrete: I recommend that you visit the site.

One of the most common weaknesses of business presentations is the use of nonconcrete or tentative language. Avoid using the frequently heard words and phrases that follow.

6

I think	I feel	I hope	I guess
I tend to think	a little	may or might	you know
kind of	perhaps	maybe	it seems
sort of	could	somewhat	

Try This

Take the list of tentative words and use each of them in a sentence. Then revise the sentences, eliminating any indication of tentativeness.

_____

_____

_____

_____

_____

_____

_____

_____

_____

(continued)

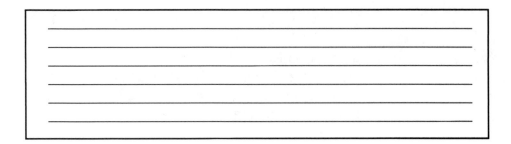

SUPPORTING TECHNIQUE 4: Be Concise

As Franklin Delano Roosevelt said, "A good speaker will be brief . . . be bright . . . be gone!"

Business speakers often make the mistake of reading speeches. Written and spoken language should be different. While long complex sentences can be seen, read, and re-read for clarity and meaning, those same sentences are hard to follow when spoken once. Be concise! Two examples follow.

Not concise:	We believe the issue at hand would benefit by immediate attention to future responses.
Concise:	We want action.
Not concise:	The lack of obfuscation and complexity combined with brevity and clarity will enhance your listeners' receptivity.
Concise:	Keep it short and simple.

Which statements are more memorable?

SUPPORTING TECHNIQUE 5: Be Consistent

Consistency means using the same language throughout a speech when you are repeatedly referring to an idea, a product, a statistic, and so on. Don't change identifying labels or terms during your speech. Business speakers frequently make the mistake of changing terminology as they move through a speech. Listeners may not recognize the change in terminology and can easily become confused.

Consistency is also important when you use visuals. Always use the same words in your speaking and in your visuals. Be consistent. Here are some examples.

Not consistent:	Federal revenue enhancers will affect transportation budgets. Financial requests should reflect these travel taxes.
Consistent:	Federal travel taxes will affect transportation budgets. Financial requests should reflect these travel taxes.
Not consistent:	Senior management has produced guidelines which reflect the changes. These recommendations should be considered the latest thinking of administration on the issue.
Consistent:	The guidelines produced by senior management reflect the current thinking on the issue.

SUPPORTING TECHNIQUE 6: Be Correct

It feels strange to say be correct. We are normally concerned with being effective.

Slang and profanity are neither correct nor effective in business speaking.

Although some businesspeople make the mistake of using slang or profanity, most of the errors we hear in business speaking break the simpler rules of grammar. The most common errors are:

Agreement in Number

Incorrect:	There is many reasons for the decline.
Correct:	There are many reasons for the decline.
Incorrect:	Insufficient numbers of staff are the chief cause of the slowdown.
Correct:	Insufficient numbers of staff is the chief cause of the slowdown.

Use of Like

Incorrect:	Like, it's one of the best tools we have. We like use it for everything. Customers like really like it, too.
Correct:	It's one of the best tools we have. We use it for everything. Customers really like it, too.
Incorrect:	I feel like I should attend the meeting.
Correct:	I feel that I should attend the meeting.
Incorrect:	Like I said before, we can't afford it.
Correct:	As I said before, we can't afford it.

(continued)

Use of Like *(continued)*

Incorrect: She sounds like she's pleased with the report.

Correct: She sounds as if she's pleased with the report.

Like should not be used before clauses or phrases. Use as, as if, as though, or that.

Mispronunciation can also be a problem among business speakers. Here is a list of frequently mispronounced words:

What We Hear		What It Should Be
Nucular	(Nuclear)	Nukleear
Aks	(Ask)	Ask
Lenth	(Length)	Length
Libary	(Library)	Library
Tetnichal	(Technical)	Technical
Recunize	(Recognize)	Recognize
Probly	(Probably)	Probably
Pitcher	(Picture)	Piccher

LEARNING ACTION PLAN

Use this form to commit to learning and practicing speaking and communication skills. In the middle column, jot down the steps you plan to take to master the skills presented. Set a date for completion of these steps.

LEARNING ACTION PLAN		
Skill: Choosing Language		
Technique	**Action to Take**	**Date Due**
1. Be clear	_____ _____	
2. Be colorful	_____ _____	
3. Be concrete	_____ _____	
4. Be concise	_____ _____	
5. Be consistent	_____ _____	
6. Be correct	_____ _____	

6

Chapter Checkpoints

Dos

✓ Do choose the most effective language for the group.

✓ Do use correct grammar.

✓ Do match the language to the level of listener understanding.

✓ Do practice saying new words out loud before you use them.

Don'ts

✓ Don't be crude. It's crass.

✓ Don't use adolescent "cool" language with adults.

✓ Don't try to sound like someone you're not. Be yourself.

✓ Don't use tentative language when you can be concrete.

CHAPTER

7 | Controlling Nonverbal Behavior

This chapter will help you to:

- Understand the importance of nonverbal behavior.
- Learn six nonverbal techniques to make your presentations more effective.

The very first impression your listeners get is nonverbal. They see how you're dressed, how you move in the room, and how comfortably and effectively you gesture. They even look at how you look at them.

A business presentation is not simply spoken. A great deal of unspoken information is always communicated. Your message is delivered over both audio and video channels. To be an effective speaker you must control both channels.

Your skill in controlling the video channel must appear completely natural. There are two golden rules for controlling nonverbal behavior:

1. Be yourself.

Be natural. Don't try to be or do something that is not natural to you.

2. Don't do anything that draws attention to itself.

In other words, try to avoid nervous gestures or fidgeting that will draw listeners away from your message.

Six techniques follow that will help you use your nonverbal behavior to your advantage rather than your detriment:

47

SUPPORTING TECHNIQUE 1: Dress

You will have to make some decisions about what style works for you. Remember, many of the messages you send are nonverbal. Your clothes may speak louder than your words.

Here are a few specific pointers:

1. Be comfortable. Be yourself. Be your professional self, not your casual, at-home, on-the-back-porch-with-friends self.
2. Be respectful. Right or wrong, some listeners will make judgments about your message based on their interpretation of the respect you are showing by your choice of dress.
3. Be careful. Dress and appearance include everything you wear, jewelry, briefcases and handbags as well as clothes. Your listeners will notice and judge your complete appearance. The best rule of thumb is simpler is safer.

7

SUPPORTING TECHNIQUE 2: Facial Expression

Nothing lights up your face like a smile. A smile is very effective in making listeners feel comfortable. Some speakers are born with a natural smile.

A smile is positive because of the warmth, friendliness, and good spirit it conveys. A smile can also be a negative if it sends this message at an inappropriate time. Have you ever been misunderstood by smiling at the wrong time?

Most people have to learn to smile when speaking to a group. It may seem strange at first, but use a mirror or video camera to practice smiling.

Even if you have been blessed with a Hollywood smile, you must use it. Adjust your attitude and set it for smile. A great smile can't overcome a sour attitude.

Try This

Using a video camera or mirror, try smiles that carry these different messages: Love, nervousness, friendship, or embarrassment. Believe it or not, smiles can be practiced and learned.

SUPPORTING TECHNIQUE 3:
Eye Contact

"The eyes are the windows of the soul." "Look me straight in the eye." "You could see it in his eyes." How many times have you heard these expressions? Your eyes are a very expressive medium for sending messages.

Other cultures may view eye contact very differently. Some even consider it rude or aggressive. Be familiar with the culture and mores of your listeners before you use eye contact. For most, eye contact between speaker and listener is positive.

As with smiling, you can send the wrong message by making or holding eye contact inappropriately. In a business presentation, eye contact should not be held for longer than four or five seconds with one person. Move on to another listener after this brief contact. This way, every listener feels more in tune with the speaker.

7

■ Try This

Choose a design such as the letter X or Z. Now, draw that design on your listeners. Move your eye contact, making that design as you speak. This invites all listeners to be included.

SUPPORTING TECHNIQUE 4:
Body Movement

Body movement, including posture, sitting, standing, and walking is an important aspect of effective speaking. It is very important that you remember golden rule 1: Be yourself.

In business speaking, it is often effective to use natural gestures as emphasis for your points. Here are three specific guidelines, but remember, follow them in your style.

1. Stand or sit erect without slouching.
2. Move slowly, two or three steps at a time.
3. Control nervous behavior such as toe-tapping, leg-swinging, jingling change, and playing with pens. Remember golden rule 2: Don't draw unwanted attention that will distract your listeners.

SUPPORTING TECHNIQUE 5:
Hand and Arm Gestures

Hand and arm gestures can be very effective in business speaking. The golden rule is: Be yourself.

Here are three specific guidelines for hand and arm gestures. Adapt them to your own style.

1. Gesture at or above the waist.
2. Keep fingers straight and pointed upward.
3. Gesture to emphasize your key points.

> **Try This**
>
> Stand in front of a mirror or videotape yourself delivering a one-minute presentation. Identify your most natural body movement and any typical nervous behaviors or gestures that could detract from your presentation. Videotaping yourself could be a painful experience, but it will help you see your most common, but correctable presentation errors.

SUPPORTING TECHNIQUE 6:
Conditions Affecting Behavior

Sometimes conditions you can't control affect your nonverbal behavior. How many times has your listening been affected by room temperature or a poor audio system? Be aware of these conditions and check them out beforehand.

1. Size of room.
2. Temperature.
3. Seating arrangements.
4. Type of furniture.
5. Time of day, week, year.
6. Lighting, acoustics.
7. Use of visual aids.
8. Location.
9. Other speakers.
10. Makeup of audience.
11. Your reputation.
12. Reason for speaking/listening.

Use this list as a checklist for your next presentation. Get information about each of these factors before you speak. Following the presentation, ask yourself if this information was helpful and in what ways it was useful.

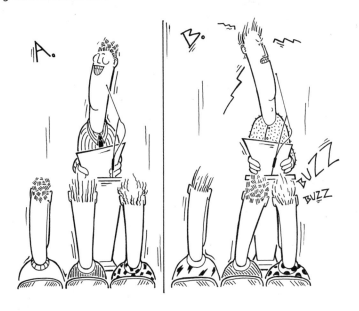

LEARNING ACTION PLAN

Use this form to commit to learning and practicing speaking and communication skills. In the middle column, jot down the steps you plan to take to master the skills presented. Set a date for completion of these steps.

LEARNING ACTION PLAN		
Skill: Controlling Nonverbal Behavior		
Technique	**Action to Take**	**Date Due**
1. Dress		
2. Facial expression		
3. Eye contact		
4. Body movement		
5. Hand and arm gestures		
6. Conditions affecting behavior		

Chapter Checkpoints

Dos

✓ Do be yourself.

✓ Do be natural.

✓ Do smile frequently.

✓ Do move eye contact around the room.

✓ Do assess environmental factors.

✓ Do check the conditions where you will be speaking.

Don'ts

✓ Don't do anything that attracts attention to itself.

✓ Don't be choreographed.

✓ Don't use unnatural gestures.

✓ Don't assume no one will notice.

8 | Using Visuals

This chapter will help you to:

- Understand the role of visual aids in a presentation.
- Learn four techniques for integrating visual aids into a presentation.

Visual aids can be handouts, slides, overheads, transparencies, videos, flip charts, models, and anything else a speaker may use to clarify or emphasize. Clarification and emphasis are the two main reasons for using visual aids during a presentation.

It's rare to attend a business presentation where visual aids are not used. Technology has increased the availability and variety of visuals, and decreased the cost of producing visuals. This is a visual age. Speakers and listeners are comfortable with and dependent on visuals. But remember:

You are not a human aid. You do not aid the visual. The visual is there to aid you.

Your visuals shouldn't be so slick and glitzy that they draw more attention than you do. Listeners should receive the information from you. Your visuals are intended to aid you. Four key supporting techniques for using visuals are covered next.

SUPPORTING TECHNIQUE 1:
Synchronization

As a speaker, you send messages to your listeners over two channels at the same time. One channel is audio, what you say. The other channel is video, what you show. Your challenge as a speaker is to synchronize the audio portion of your message with the video to present one synchronized message and thereby keep your listener in sync with you. You want your listener to be reacting to your message when and in the way you have planned. To achieve synchronization show your visual exactly when you are talking about the point on the visual. When you're finished covering that one point take the corresponding visual away. This will keep your listeners in sync with you and your message.

The most important rule for ensuring synchronization is: one point per visual.

You may know speakers who prefer to include several points on a single visual. This type of visual is easier to produce and can be used as an outline for the speaker. Just as it allows the speaker to read ahead, such a visual also allows the listener to read ahead and this should be avoided. When the listener reads ahead of the speaker, both parties are out of sync and the message may be lost.

SUPPORTING TECHNIQUE 2:
Introduction

8

Before showing any visual to your listeners, introduce it. Depending on the purpose and complexity of the visual, your introduction can be as short as a few words or as long as several sentences. The purpose of the introduction is to prepare your listeners and ensure that they will focus on the visual.

If you do not orient and prepare your listeners for a visual, the listeners will be forced to scan, review, and analyze the visual while you are speaking. All this activity detracts from speaker-listener synchronization.

Remember: It's the listener you're trying to please, it's the listener you're trying to persuade, and it's the listener you're trying to impress. That doesn't mean that, as a speaker, using visuals has to be difficult. It does mean you need to practice techniques to aid the listener. Introducing visuals and allowing only one point per visual do precisely that.

Here are a few sample introductions for visuals:

1. "The next visual is a pie chart that shows. . . ."

2. "This list of cities includes. . . ."

3. "The next three visuals are diagrams of. . . ."

Try This

Create and videotape a two-minute presentation by selecting a topic from the front page of the business section of your paper. Use at least three visuals during the presentation. Prepare an outline for the audio portion of your presentation and indicate on that outline precisely where your visuals will be used. As you review your video, ask the following questions:

1. Have I allowed only one point per visual?

2. Have I introduced each visual before showing it?

3. Are my audio and video channels synchronized?

Becoming aware of your common errors with visuals is the first step toward correcting your mistakes.

SUPPORTING TECHNIQUE 3:
Set-up

You may find it necessary to use a complex visual that contains more information or detail than you actually want to discuss. Examples include maps, equations, diagrams, blueprints, lists, or photographs that say more than you want to talk about. You may want to focus only on a single aspect or particular portion of this type of visual. If you cannot simplify the visual, it's time to use a technique called *set-up*. Set-up is telling your listeners exactly which part of a visual you want them to focus on.

For example:

1. "On this next graph, please direct your attention to the yellow line on the right side of the graph."

2. "The next blueprint is somewhat complicated, so please focus your attention on the upper left corner of the blueprint."

3. "The next visual contains a list of cities. We will be most concerned about those highlighted in red."

Try This ———————————————————

Imagine a photograph of your home. Before showing the photograph to a friend, describe which portion of the photograph contains the front door.

Then take a page from a magazine. Before showing your friend the page, describe a specific ad located at the bottom left corner of the page. This will get you in the habit of focusing on a portion of a complex image—a skill that can be transferred to your use of visuals.

SUPPORTING TECHNIQUE 4: Talk and Do

When you use visuals, you also need to flip charts, change overhead transparencies, and move other visuals while you're speaking. Listeners appreciate a prepared and coordinated speaker, who can confidently coordinate speaking with all the activity involved in using visuals.

Does all this sound almost silly to you? "Of course, I can talk and do something else at the same time." Don't be so sure. How many times have you seen a speaker fumbling with a flip chart, using upside-down overheads, or tickling a tape recorder to make it work?

It is disruptive when a speaker stops or changes the rhythm of a presentation to manipulate the visuals. To ensure a smooth transmission of thoughts and information, you must practice the physical skills needed to handle visuals.

1. Is the flip chart at a height that is comfortable for flipping pages?
2. Do you know how to turn on, fast forward, rewind, or pause the tape recorder?
3. Is your handwriting legible?

Try This ———————————————————

Prepare a two-minute presentation. Use three different visual forms and videotape it. Review the tape. If you or an observer hardly notice the way you handle the visuals, you've already developed some comfort level with visuals. If not, make an effort to practice until you feel at ease. Be honest with yourself—do these problems interfere with your presentation?

LEARNING ACTION PLAN

Use this form to commit to learning and practicing speaking and communication skills. In the middle column, jot down the steps you plan to take to master the skills presented. Set a date for completion of these steps.

LEARNING ACTION PLAN		
Skill: Using Visuals		
Technique	**Action to Take**	**Date Due**
1. Synchronization		
2. Introduction		
3. Set-up		
4. Talk and do		

Chapter Checkpoints

Dos

✓ Do let your visuals aid you.

✓ Do use visuals to clarify and emphasize.

✓ Do stay in sync with your listeners.

✓ Do make one point per visual.

✓ Do introduce each visual before showing it.

✓ Do practice handling your visuals ahead of time.

Don'ts

✓ Don't hide behind your visuals.

✓ Don't let technology or visuals be more interesting than you.

✓ Don't use visuals as detailed notes.

✓ Don't interrupt your presentation by fumbling with your visuals.

CHAPTER

9 | Handling Questions

This chapter will help you to:

- Understand the value of questions.
- Learn four techniques for handling questions.

Questions? Some speakers love them, some speakers hate them. Love them or hate them, you're going to get them. Listeners like to ask questions. It's as simple as that. As a speaker, you need to know the best way to react.

First, how do you handle those occasions when you don't want any questions? At the beginning of your presentation, you tell the listeners that questions:

- Are to be submitted in writing.
- Will be answered privately.
- Can be asked later.

Remember that almost all presentations will elicit questions. Frankly, many speakers welcome questions as a method to encourage interaction and to take the focus away from themselves for a brief moment. Questions can be an opportunity to project a confident, competent impression.

Here are four techniques that will help you respond more effectively to questions.

SUPPORTING TECHNIQUE 1:
Encouraging Questions

Most listeners are shy about asking questions. They may be shy about speaking in front of the group, or worry about appearing stupid. They may not be sure about exactly how or what to ask. On the other hand, you'll always find people for whom none of this is true. Some people would ask anything.

For most listeners, you have to tell them that asking questions is encouraged and perhaps even ask them to ask questions. Then you will have to ask them again, and tell them again several times. You may have to provide the right environment for questions. For example, you might say:

1. "I will be very happy to take your questions during the presentations."
2. "Remember, I invite your questions at any time."
3. "As I said earlier, I welcome your questions, so please feel free to ask whatever you'd like."

However, never say: "Please feel free to interrupt me with any questions you'd like to ask." We have all been taught that interrupting is rude. A more pleasant and productive way to elicit questions is to say something like:

1. "What questions do you have?"
2. "I'm certain there are many questions and I look forward to hearing each of them. What questions do you have about what I've said?"

SUPPORTING TECHNIQUE 2:
Listening to the Question

Why do listeners ask questions? Their reasons may include any of the following:

- To get information.
- To give information.
- To impress other listeners.

- To think out loud.
- To trip you up.

Sometimes these reasons are obvious; sometimes they are hidden. As a speaker, you shouldn't automatically think every questioner has a hidden agenda. Take the question at face value and answer it as directly as you can.

Here are a few guidelines on how to listen to questions.

1. Get ready to listen.
2. Pay attention. Stop thinking about what your next presentation point will be. Don't fumble through your notes or visuals. Establish eye contact with the questioner. Get ready and pay attention.
3. Control your biases. This may be very difficult, but try not to allow your biases toward the questioner to get in the way of your ability to pay attention and formulate a response.
4. Separate fact from feeling. Listen carefully for words or statements that indicate whether the speaker is questioning based on emotions or based on facts. This difference, will, of course, color your response.
5. Don't interrupt the questioner. Listen to the entire question before responding.

SUPPORTING TECHNIQUE 3: Responding to Questions

When is the appropriate time to respond to questions? On one hand, you should answer questions when they are asked. On the other hand, this could be very disruptive. Before the presentation, decide whether you would like to accept questions as you proceed or when you've finished.

When a question is asked, it is often helpful to restate or paraphrase the question for other listeners who may not have heard the questioner. This also gives you a few moments to think about your answer.

If the question is inappropriate, off the topic, or misleading, ask the questioner to clarify, restate, justify, or relate the question to your points in the speech. Three words of advice: Don't be defensive.

Treat your questioners with the same respect, patience, and under-standing you projected in your speech delivery. In addition thank questioners for asking. Your thanks will ensure that others feel safe and comfortable in asking their questions.

SUPPORTING TECHNIQUE 4:
How to Say "I Don't Know"

For politicians, "I don't know" may be the three deadliest words in the English language. But politicians aren't the only people who have trouble saying these three simple words. Many speakers face this difficulty. On one hand, they want to appear confident and competent. On the other hand, they may not know the answer to a tricky question.

So what should a speaker do? **Tell the truth.** Remember what Shake-speare noted: "Oh what a tangled web we weave when first we practice to deceive."

If you do not know the answer to a question, you have several options:

- Admit your lack of knowledge and offer to do research and respond later.
- Ask other listeners for help in providing the necessary information.
- Ask questioners to expand on their questions and explain their reasons for asking.
- Offer to discuss the question during break time or at the conclusion of your presentation.

LEARNING ACTION PLAN

Use this form to commit to learning and practicing speaking and communication skills. In the middle column, jot down the steps you plan to take to master the skills presented. Set a date for completion of these steps.

LEARNING ACTION PLAN		
Skill: Handling Questions		
Technique	**Action to Take**	**Date Due**
1. Encouraging questions	_____ _____	
2. Listening to the question	_____ _____	
3. Responding to questions	_____ _____	
4. How to say, "I don't know"	_____ _____	

9

Chapter Checkpoints

Dos

✓ Do expect questions.

✓ Do listen to questions carefully.

✓ Do repeat questions when appropriate.

✓ Do respond to questions briefly.

✓ Do thank people for questions.

Don'ts

✓ Don't avoid questions.

✓ Don't interrupt the questioner.

✓ Don't be defensive.

✓ Don't change your speaking style when answering questions.

✓ Don't hesitate to ask other listeners for assistance in answering questions.

10 | The Final Touch

This chapter will help you to:

- Understand the importance of getting started, both with your preparation and with your presentation.
- Learn five techniques for getting started.

Here are five supporting techniques to help you put the final touches on your presentation: clothing, diet and fitness, using notes, openings, and practicing.

SUPPORTING TECHNIQUE 1: Clothing

We've covered this at some length in Chapter 7, but this topic is important enough for a second look. Before your listeners listen to you, they look at you. They begin to make judgments and draw conclusions based on your appearance.

Make sure your appearance presents the same tone you convey in your speech. Above all:

1. Be yourself.
2. Don't wear anything that speaks louder than you.
3. Respect your listeners' tastes.
4. Wear comfortable clothing.
5. Understate rather than overstate your style.
6. Don't fidget with hair and jewelry.

SUPPORTING TECHNIQUE 2: Diet and Fitness

When you feel fit, you speak better; you are more enthusiastic and communicate greater sincerity and confidence. Believe it or not, your diet and exercise can affect your speaking performance. The checklist below provides guidelines for staying in top speaking condition.

Fitness Checklist	Check When Completed

1. Exercise regularly. We suggest walking 30 minutes, three times a week to get your breathing steady and regular.

2. Practice headrolls five times daily. Keep your lower jaw relaxed and roll your head in a slow circle. If you practice this directly before a presentation, you'll relax your neck and voice muscles.

3. Stretch arms over your head and swing them side to side. Do this stretching throughout the day and one minute prior to presenting. These stretches help reduce tension.

4. Do deep knee bends throughout the day. Do three of them prior to speaking and you'll feel more relaxed and comfortable before speaking.

5. Avoid dairy products on the day of your presentation. They cause a harmless but annoying congestion around your vocal cords.

6. Avoid alcohol and drugs before presenting. They can dull your senses.

7. Avoid smoking. It debilitates breathing and impairs blood supply to the brain.

8. Avoid carbonated drinks. They promote burping.

10

SUPPORTING TECHNIQUE 3: Using Notes

There is no magic formula for using notes. Some speakers like them, others don't. Some speakers use detailed notes; some speakers use a brief outline. What works for you? Our preference and recommendation is: **Follow the KISS method: Keep It Short and Simple.**

Generally speaking, notes are intended to guide and remind the speaker. Whatever format you choose, be sure your notes don't come between you and your listeners. For preparing and using notes we recommend:

1. Notes should be notes. Do not write your notes in sentence form.

2. Notes should be easy to see. Write them large enough and dark enough to see at a glance.

3. Never read notes to your listeners. Use notes to remind and guide yourself not your listeners.

4. Note cards (3X5) are easy to handle. They are also inconspicuous.

5. Put no more than two notations on a note card.

6. Each notation should prompt at least 30 seconds of speaking time.

SUPPORTING TECHNIQUE 4: Openings

The opening of any speech is highly important. Should it be direct, erudite, humorous, clever, or rhetorical? Any of these openings could be appropriate and effective. Choose an opening that fits your style, the event, the topic, and the listeners' style. Do you remember the time you heard a speaker open with a joke that bombed, or told a funny story that wasn't funny? **Appropriateness is a key to effectiveness.**

Here are five proven successful openings:

1. Refer to the previous speaker.   Refer to the speaker's style, wit, or reputation. Refer to the previous speaker's topic.

2. Ask a question.   Perhaps you should ask two or three questions. If you want responses tell your listeners this. If you open with rhetorical questions, say so, and answer them during your presentation.

3. Use a shocking statement.   It should catch listeners' attention. It should not be offensive.

4. Refer to the situation, the setting, or the location.

5. Use humor and anecdotes.   Always use self-deprecating humor. Never poke fun at other people's expense. Use anecdotes that are short and clever, cute, humorous, or relevant to your topic.

10

SUPPORT TECHNIQUE 5: Practicing

Practicing means just that. There is no magic number of repetitions for successful practice. Some speakers can practice their presentation once and they're done. Other speakers must practice and practice and practice until moments before they begin.

How often should you practice? The answer will vary with the speaker.

Here are a few guidelines for practicing:

1. Practice out loud. Get accustomed to the sound and feel of the words in your presentation.

2. Audio- and/or videotape your practice session. Whenever possible, review the tape as a listener, without your notes.

3. Practice in segments. When using the four-step outline, practice each step as a separate segment. (See Chapter 3 if you need to refresh your understanding of the four-step outline.) Don't proceed to the next segment until you are pleased with the one you are practicing.

4. Ask a coach, colleague, or friend to listen and provide feedback and criticism. Urge them to be specific and completely honest.

5. Practice answers to possible questions. Think of the easiest and the most difficult questions you might be asked and practice your answer.

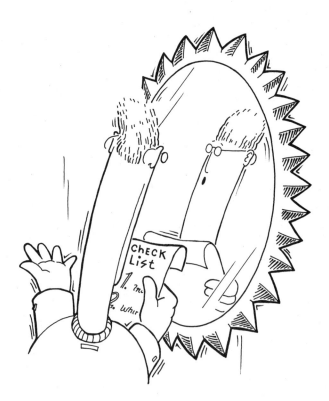

LEARNING ACTION PLAN

Use this form to commit to learning and practicing speaking and communication skills. In the middle column, jot down the steps you plan to take to master the skills presented. Set a date for completion of these steps.

LEARNING ACTION PLAN		
Skill: Adding the Final Touches		
Technique	**Action to Take**	**Date Due**
1. Clothing	_____ _____	
2. Diet and fitness	_____ _____	
3. Using notes	_____ _____	
4. Openings	_____ _____	
5. Practicing	_____ _____	

10

Chapter Checkpoints

Dos

✓ Do be physically prepared for your presentation.

✓ Do keep your notes simple.

✓ Do choose the appropriate opening for each speaking event.

✓ Do practice out loud.

Don'ts

✓ Don't count on a second chance to make a first impression.

✓ Don't ignore your psychological and physiological needs for preparation.

✓ Don't write notes in sentence form.

✓ Don't use an opening just because it worked for someone else.

✓ Don't rush through your practice.

✓ Don't over-practice. Save some enthusiasm and energy for the presentation.

Post-Tests

Now that you've completed the book, it's time to measure your improvement. As in the preliminary assessments, work with a friend to assess your view of your own progress first, then assess the speaking impression you make on a listener.

1. Speaker Post-Test

For each of the 25 statements, simply place a check (✓) in the column that most accurately describes you when you prepare and give a presentation.

	Almost Never	Some-times	Usually	Almost Always
1. I feel comfortable and relaxed when I speak to groups.	_____	_____	_____	_____
2. I avoid negative thoughts about speaking to groups.	_____	_____	_____	_____
3. My voice is even and calm, not shaky, throughout my presentation.	_____	_____	_____	_____
4. My body is relaxed while speaking.	_____	_____	_____	_____
5. I research my listeners' expectations before speaking.	_____	_____	_____	_____
6. I control the behavior of listeners throughout the presentation.	_____	_____	_____	_____
7. I elicit interaction with my listeners.	_____	_____	_____	_____
8. I use notes to organize and remind me of points to make.	_____	_____	_____	_____
9. My notes are simple, easy to read, and not disruptive to use.	_____	_____	_____	_____
10. I avoid using a word-for-word script.	_____	_____	_____	_____
11. I practice my presentation ahead of time.	_____	_____	_____	_____
12. I present benefits of listening to my listeners.	_____	_____	_____	_____
13. I use an appropriate opening to get my listeners' attention.	_____	_____	_____	_____
14. I use clear articulation.	_____	_____	_____	_____

	Almost Never	Some-times	Usually	Almost Always
15. I adjust my volume for the situation.	_____	_____	_____	_____
16. I use vocal variety to express ideas and emphasize ideas.	_____	_____	_____	_____
17. I prepare my visuals to clarify or emphasize my points.	_____	_____	_____	_____
18. My visuals are simple and readable.	_____	_____	_____	_____
19. I use natural gestures.	_____	_____	_____	_____
20. I consciously maintain eye contact with my listeners.	_____	_____	_____	_____
21. I anticipate questions and practice answering them.	_____	_____	_____	_____
22. I use appropriate language.	_____	_____	_____	_____
23. I am in control of the pacing of the presentation.	_____	_____	_____	_____
24. I stay within the allocated time frame.	_____	_____	_____	_____
25. I practice out loud and with a tape recorder.	_____	_____	_____	_____
Column Totals				
Grand Total				

To score: Give yourself one point for each check (✓) under Almost Never, two points for Sometimes, three points for Usually, and four points for Almost Always. Total each column. Then add the totals of all four columns together to get a grand total. How did you do?

100–90	Very good
89–75	Good
74–50	Average
49–30	Poor
29–0	Very poor

2. Observer Post-Test

Use this scale to assess the speaker's effectiveness in preparing a presentation and speaking to groups. Observe and listen as the speaker gives a presentation. For each of the 25 statements, simply place a check in the column that most accurately describes the speaker.

	Almost Never	Some-times	Usually	Almost Always
1. Appears comfortable and relaxed when speaking.				
2. Seems generally confident about speaking.				
3. Uses an even and calm, not shaky, speaking voice.				
4. Looks physically relaxed while speaking.				
5. Seems prepared to meet listeners' expectations.				
6. Controls listener behavior throughout the presentation.				
7. Generates interaction with listeners.				
8. Uses notes to organize and guide the presentation.				
9. Uses notes in a nondisruptive manner.				
10. Avoids using a word-for-word script.				
11. Practices presentations before speaking.				
12. Tells listeners the benefits of listening.				
13. Uses an appropriate opening to get listeners' attention.				

	Almost Never	Some-times	Usually	Almost Always
14. Uses clear articulation.	_____	_____	_____	_____
15. Adjusts volume to fit the situation.	_____	_____	_____	_____
16. Uses vocal variety to express and emphasize ideas.	_____	_____	_____	_____
17. Uses visuals to clarify or emphasize points.	_____	_____	_____	_____
18. Uses simple, easy-to-read visuals.	_____	_____	_____	_____
19. Uses natural gestures.	_____	_____	_____	_____
20. Has good eye contact.	_____	_____	_____	_____
21. Seems prepared for listeners' questions.	_____	_____	_____	_____
22. Uses appropriate language.	_____	_____	_____	_____
23. Controls the pace of the presentation.	_____	_____	_____	_____
24. Stays within the time frame.	_____	_____	_____	_____
25. Practices out loud and with a tape recorder.	_____	_____	_____	_____
Column Totals				
Grand Total				

To score: Give the speaker one point for each check (✓) under Almost Never, two points for Sometimes, three points for Usually, and four points for Almost Always. Total each column. Then add the totals of all four columns together to get a grand total.

100–90	Very good
89–75	Good
74–50	Average
49–30	Poor
29–0 0	Very poor

THE BUSINESS SKILLS EXPRESS SERIES

This growing series of books addresses a broad range of key business skills and topics to meet the needs of employees, human resource departments, and training consultants.

To obtain information about these and other Business Skills Express books, please call Business One IRWIN toll free at: 1-800-634-3966.